Cody Just can't Help it!

&

The Worst Day Ever for a Third Grader!

WRITTEN BY DEREK GIBSON
ILLUSTRATED BY AADIL KHAN

Printed in the United States of America

ISBN: 9798330435036

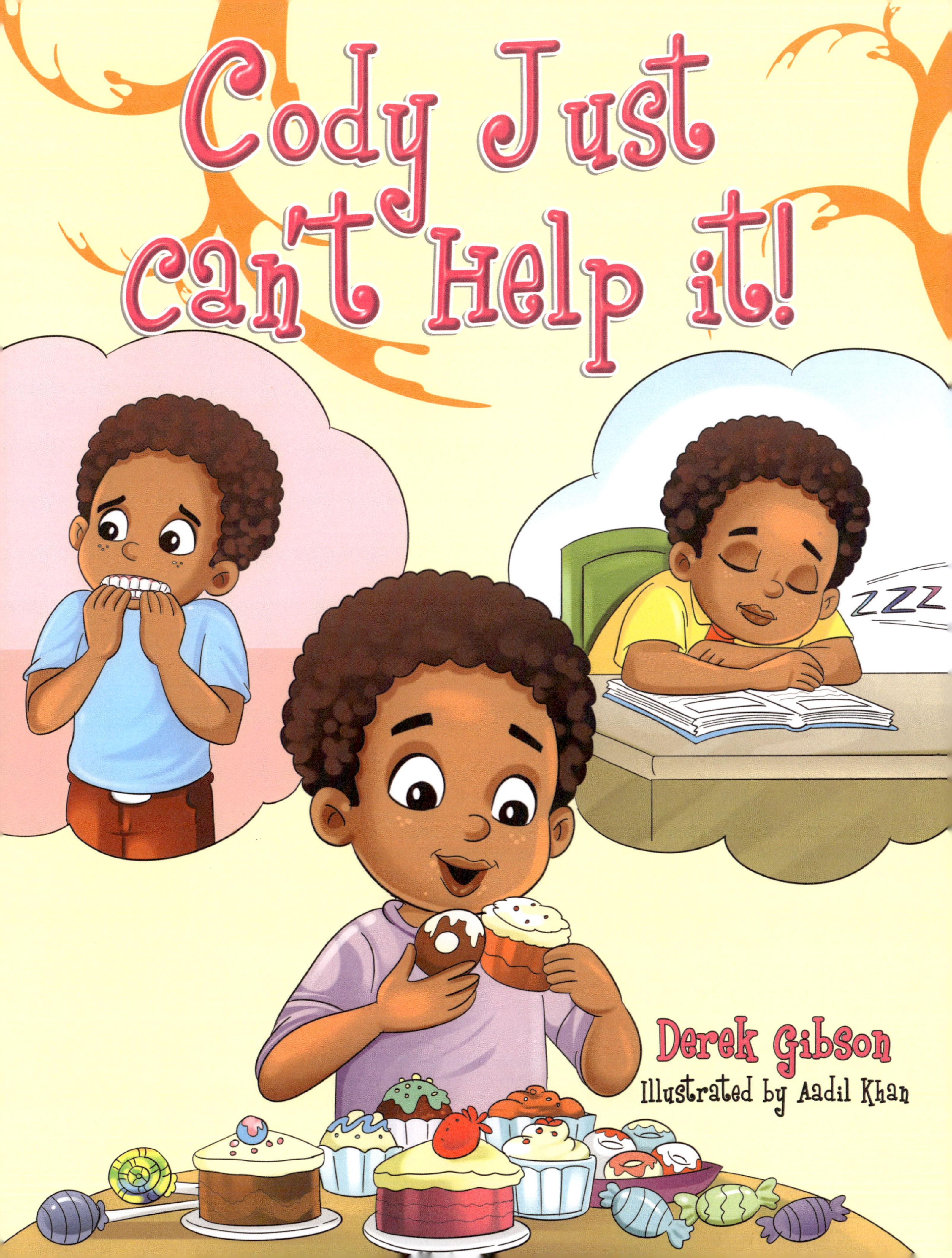

Cody Just Can't Help it!
Derek Gibson
Illustrated by Aadil Khan
ZZZ

Cody Just Can't Help it!

WRITTEN BY DEREK GIBSON

ILLUSTRATED BY AADIL KHAN

Print ISBN: 9798869298577
eBook ISBN: 9798869298584

This book is dedicated to YOU
and kids everywhere who work hard
to break their bad habits.
Bad habits can be broken, and good habits can
change your future for the better.
- Author, Derek Gibson

@sodik_diki
45+21=
4 X 8 =
NO.1
math
BE HAPPY
Smile Everyday
Good Job!
2 X 2
7
4
5
Smile

4

Cody Skittle is like any other second grader.

He loves video games, reading comic books, and playing on the school soccer team, "The Titans."

Cody is also nice and friendly, always willing to lend a helping hand.

Sometimes, he will even help his teacher clean the blackboard after class.

All his teachers call him their little A+ helper.

But like every kid, Cody was not perfect.

About that make no mistake.

He just had a few bad habits he desperately
needed to break.

Cody has so many bad habits, he can even count
them on two hands.

No matter how hard he tried, breaking his bad
habits was the hardest thing to do.

Maybe **YOU** can help give Cody some advice on
why he should break these bad habits.

Hey there,
Can you help me break a
few of my bad habits?

Cody loves to eat...and eat...and eat. He eats everything and sometimes he doesn't know when to stop.

Cookies, candy, cupcakes, and chocolate - you name it.

Those are his four favorite foods in the whole world. He could eat them all day and night.

He would even sneak his favorite snacks under his bed whenever he thought no one was looking, and that's not right.

He was always afraid someone would take it away if they saw him snacking all the time.

He always ate more than he would ever admit.

But he didn't care. No, not at all.

Cody just can't help it.

He thought eating his favorite foods just meant he would grow up to be very strong and tall.

Let's tell Code that too much of anything is never a good idea.

And eating so much unhealthy foods is very bad for your health and even bad for your teeth.

Cody also NEVER liked to wash his hands.

Not even before he ate his breakfast,

Not even before eating his dinner...or even before feeding his baby brother.

Sometimes, he doesn't wash his hands after he picks his nose!

EWWWWWWW, GROSS!!!

Can we also tell Cody that picking his nose is a bad habit too? Can someone get Cody some tissues so he can blow his nose?

GO AWAY!!!

He didn't care. **CODY just Can't help it.**

Not washing his hands and picking his nose are two bad habits Cody should definitely break. Germs can make us all sick! They can spread from one person to another faster than you can say 1,2,3!

Let's tell Cody that washing our hands is important to keep those ugly, nasty, disgusting germs away.

Cody always liked to watch cartoons with the TV way too loud!

"Cody, the TV is too loud!!! Please turn it down!" his father would yell constantly.

Code can never hear him because the TV is blaring too loudly.

The TV is so loud, even Jaxon the dog covers his ears.

BUT CODY JUST COULDN'T HELP IT.

Watching cartoons with the volume loud was fun for him...even if it was painful to listen to.

Blaring noise can cause damage to our ear drums, especially if we aren't careful.

Let's remind Cody to break this habit now before he begins to have trouble hearing.

Cody loved to bite his nails. Sometimes he would chew his nails and spit them out all over the place. It was one of his worst habits, not to mention one of the hardest for him to break.

But Cody just couldn't help it!

Biting his nails always calmed him down, especially before it was time for him to bat at his little league game.

Can someone tell Cody that biting his nails may lead to skin infections, chipped teeth and damage to your nails. It may also cause nasty bacteria to enter your mouth and none of us would want that!

Let's also tell Cody to try his best to relax and stay calm so he can hit a home run!

Cody always sneaks out of his bed late at night to play video games.

"It's a school night Cody. Go to sleep this instant or I'm telling mom!" his older sister shouted, overhearing him from the hallway.

"Just five more minutes, Natalie!" said Cody.

Cody would play his games for hours and hours. Sometimes until the next morning. He would barely get any sleep at all.

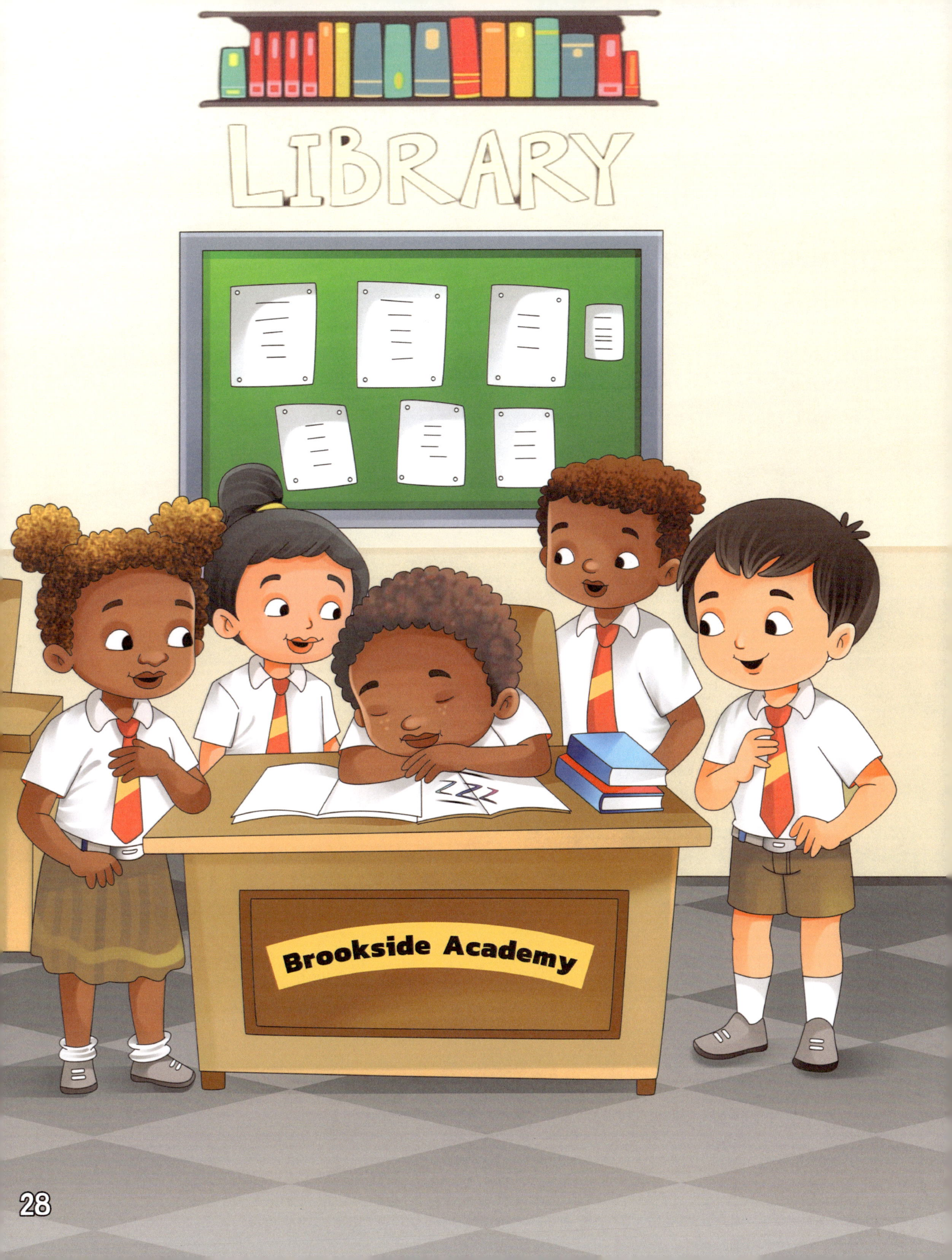
LIBRARY
ZZZ
Brookside Academy

Sometimes, he would even fall asleep during class.

Once, he was caught sleeping in the library.

Sometimes, kids would stare and giggle as if he was an alien from outer space.

Cody would even miss the school bell at the end of the day.

Cody just couldn't help it.

Can someone please tell Cody how important sleep is for everyone? Sleep helps us function and do our best. Sleep is also great for our health. Cody should understand that it's not good to stay up late to play video games on a school night. Maybe Cody should also listen to his parents and go to sleep when he is told, even if he is not sleepy. Perhaps he should try counting sheep.

1 sheep, 2 sheep, 3 sheep...

Cody never liked to clean his room.

His mother would remind him to clean his room every day, but he always made up some excuse not to.

Cody's room is always a BIG MESS!!! It always looks like a tornado destroyed it.

There are things everywhere...toys, clothes, balls, board games, food, even his pet turtle.

It's so messy he can never find anything he is looking for.

Sometimes he can't even find his dog, Jaxon.

Cody would sometimes be late to school because he could never find his backpack.

By now, we all know, Cody just can't help it!

Let's tell Cody that his life would be a lot easier
if he would learn to put everything in its proper
place.

Let's face it. Being a kid is hard work isn't it?

Let's hope Cody takes our advice and tries to
break these bad habits for good.

Maybe Cody helped you think about breaking some
of your own bad habits.

Some habits are very hard to break and
sometimes we might need help from others when
it gets really tough. Ultimately, it's all up to you.
Try it. You can do it too!

What bad habits are you trying to break?

Maybe you can help someone break their bad habits too.

Wouldn't it be amazing if we could break them once and for all?

Try your best to break one of your terrible habits today if you can.

Just take it one day at a time. You'll be so glad you did.

Thanks for reading.

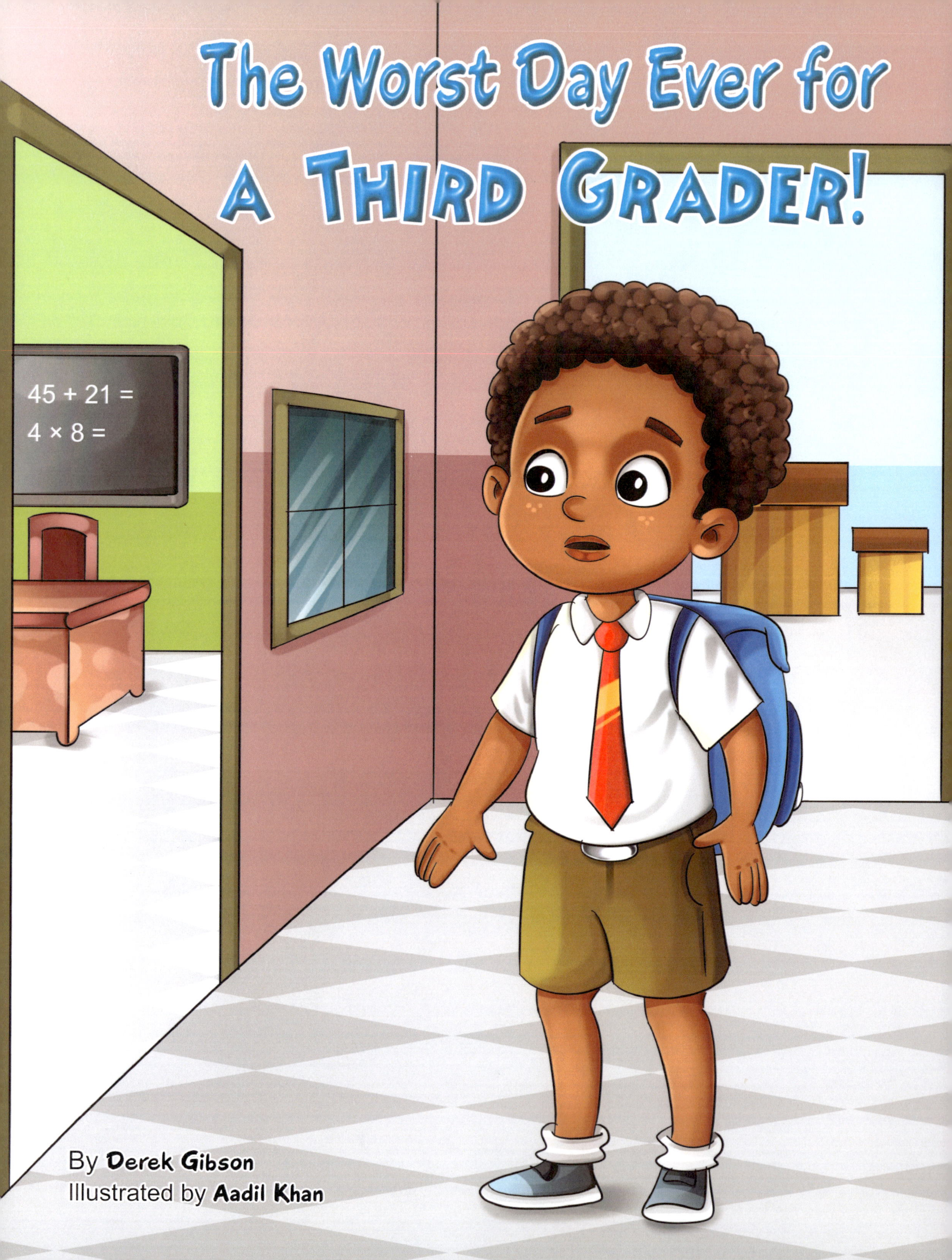
45 + 21 =
4 × 8 =
The Worst Day Ever for A Third Grader!
By Derek Gibson
Illustrated by Aadil Khan

*To all the kids who recently
survived their worst day ever.*

If you're having a bad day, just remember
that you managed to get through every
bad day you've had so far.

You'll make it through this one too.

The Worst Day Ever for a Third Grader!

WRITTEN BY DEREK GIBSON
ILLUSTRATED BY AADIL KHAN

It was the first day of the third grade for
Cody Skittle. He was so excited! He dashed out
of bed as soon as the alarm clock woke him
up. Cody got ready, brushed his teeth, threw
on his backpack and headed towards the
door. His mother kissed him goodbye and off
he went. He wanted to make sure he wasn't
late for his first day in the third grade.

On the way to the bus stop, Cody stepped in a big puddle of mud.

"Oh no!" said Cody. There was mud all over his clothes.

"Now I'm dirty and I'm going to be late to school," Cody complained.

He hurried back home.

BUS-STOP

"What happened to you?" asked his mother.

"I stepped in a big puddle of mud on my way to the bus stop," he said with a frown.

"Let's hurry and get you out of these dirty clothes," said his mother as she took his hand and hurried him back to his room to change.

Cody grabbed his backpack and hurried out the door once again. He ran even faster than before.

He was definitely not going to miss the bus on a day like today.

As Cody got closer to the bus stop, he noticed the bus leaving.

"WAAAAAAIT!!...WAAAAAAAAIT!!!!, shouted Cody as he ran after the bus.

It was too late. The bus was too far ahead.

"THIS DAY SUCKS SO FAR," said Cody.

SCHOOL BUS
WAAAITT...

Cody hurried back home again.

"Mom, I missed the bus. Can you drive me to school? I don't want to be late for my first day in the third grade," said Cody.

"Yes, I'll take you. Let's leave now," said his mother.

Cody and his mother quickly got in the car, but when she tried to turn it on, it wouldn't start. She tried again with no luck at all.

"Awe shucks! Not again! We won't be able to drive the car until I take it to a mechanic later today," said his mother. Getting to school on time was not looking good for Cody.

"THIS IS DEFINITELY NOT A GOOD DAY AT ALL," murmured Cody.

"I guess you will have to ride your bike to school," said his mother.

Luckily, Cody's school, Brookside Academy, was just a few blocks away. Cody got on his bike and hurried off to school. He peddled and peddled as fast as he could. He was riding so fast, it seemed like he was riding on air.

A few minutes later, Cody finally arrived.

"Thank goodness! I made it," he said with a sigh of relief.

When Cody got to his classroom, all the kids were already seated. He knew he was late because his new teacher, Mrs. Robinson was in the middle of reading over the classwork assignment. The teacher scolded Cody for being late.

"Hello, you must be Cody Skittle. You are very late young man so you must sit in the back of the classroom until class is over," said Mrs. Robinson.

Cody never thought his new teacher would be so upset. After all, it was only his first day.

Cody felt very awkward. Some of the kids whispered and teased him as he walked towards the back of the classroom. Some of them even laughed and stared at him.

This didn't make Cody feel good at all.

Cody had to sit in the back of the classroom all day long.

Later, during lunch time, Cody realized he forgot to pack his lunch.

He didn't have any lunch money to buy food from the cafeteria so he asked his friend Abby for one of her snacks. He always liked the food in Abby's lunchbox.

"Abby, can I have some of your peanut butter cookies?" asked Cody.

"Sorry Cody, I'm too hungry," said Abby.

Cody noticed his friend Allen had two apple juice boxes.

"Can I have a juice box Allen?" asked Cody.

"Sure," said Allen as he handed Cody one of the juice boxes.

Cody was so happy he had a friend like Allen who loved to share as much as he did.

Cody wanted more but he was too afraid to ask for it. Cody went all day without anything to eat.

His stomach was growling very loudly all through reading class too. So loud, some kids even thought there was an invisible growling monster in the classroom.

"CAN THIS DAY GET ANY WORSE?" Cody thought to himself.

عصير
عصير

At recess, Cody played hide and seek with his friends.

When it was time for him to hide, he stumbled over a big rock and tumbled to the ground.

Cody was so embarrassed that he fell in front of his friends.

"I AM SO OVER THIS DAY," frowned Cody.

The school bell rang and it was time for everyone to return to class.

Cody was so glad recess was finally over. He was hoping all of his friends forgot about the terrible fall he had earlier.

On the way back to class, Cody ran through the hallway so fast he accidentally crashed into Katie.

"Cody, you made me drop all of my books on the floor. Can you please stop running in the hallway?" Katie asked.

"I'm sorry Katie, I just don't want to be late back to class," said Cody.

He kept apologizing over and over again.

To make matters worse, Cody suddenly remembered he forgot to tell his mom to sign the permission slip so he could attend the upcoming "Welcome Back to School Pizza Party" on Friday. The school sent a letter about the party over the summer and it was due on the first day back to school.

"THIS IS PROBABLY THE WORST DAY EVER FOR A THIRD GRADER," said Cody as he made his way back to class.

When Mrs. Robinson was going over Math problems on the board, she called Cody to the front of the board to solve the problem.

"Cody do you know the answer?" asked Mrs. Robinson.

Cody froze. His mind went blank. He couldn't think of the answer.

All he could think about was how he stepped in mud earlier, how he missed the bus, how hungry he is, how humiliated he was at recess and how he made Katie drop all of her books.

All the kids stared at him....again.

Mrs. Robinson thought Cody was taking too long to answer so she told him to go sit back down in the back of the classroom.

"YES! THIS IS DEFINITELY THE WORST DAY EVER FOR A THIRD GRADER," thought Cody as he returned to his seat with his face buried in his hands.

7 X 50 =

After school was over, Cody rode his bike
home as quickly as he could, hoping to erase
this awful day from his memory.

BUT THEN...Cody crashed his bike into the mail
man.

There was mail scattered everywhere.

The mail man was very upset. Cody apologized
at least ten times.

Once Cody arrived home, his mom asked him about his day.

"How was your first day as a third grader, Cody?" she asked.

"I HAD THE WORST DAY EVER!" shouted Cody.

"I'm sorry you had a bad day, sweetheart. Sometimes a big hug helps," she said as she reached in to give Cody a big hug and a kiss.

"Remember, everyone has bad days. Sometimes things happen that makes us very upset. The next time you get angry or frustrated, just remember to pause for a second and take deep breaths. It helps us to calm down. You can always learn from your mistakes so you can make better decisions next time. It also helps to talk about how you feel with a friend or you can always talk to me. Talking things out usually makes us feel a lot better.

"Thanks mom," I am starting to feel better already," smiled Cody.

If you're having a bad day, just remember that you were able to get through every bad day you've had so far. You will make it through this one too," his mother said.

The next day, Cody wasn't so excited about going to school. All he could think about was the bad day he had the day before. After he got ready for school, Cody walked to the bus stop.

He didn't step in any mud. He didn't get his clothes dirty. He caught the bus on time and he was able to get to school without being late.

His mom even remembered to pack his lunch today. She even packed extra food in his lunchbox so he shared it with Abby and Allen since they forgot their lunch.

Later in math class, Mrs. Robinson called Cody to the front of the classroom to answer another multiplication problem. This time, he solved the math problem quicker than anyone else in the class and he was the only one who got it right.

Mrs. Robinson was so impressed that she gave Cody her golden star for the day.

"What a SUPER job you did today Cody," said Mrs. Robinson.

Cody was so proud of himself. Mrs. Robinson even allowed him to sit in his favorite seat...at the front of the class.

Cody was having such a great day. He spent his entire recess telling funny jokes to all his friends.

Cody was finally having his BEST DAY EVER!

The Worst
Day Ever For a
THIRD GRADER

Hello readers,

I hope you enjoyed my books

"CODY JUST CAN'T HELP IT" and

"THE WORST DAY EVER FOR A THIRD GRADER"

as much as I did writing them.

I would love to know your feedback.

Please search for them on Amazon.com and leave a REVIEW.

Recommend these books to all your friends as well.

THANK YOU SO MUCH!

Author, Derek Gibson

9 798330 435036